A Sausage Book

Would you keep man's temper sweet?
Give him tasty things to eat;
Would you still preserve your own?
Use the wisest methods known.
Variety is the charm of life,
Monotony the cause of strife.
Give your choice the widest range
As the varied season's change,
Then you'll both have tempers sweet,
And enjoy the things you eat.

from *The Everyday Savoury Book*

LUDLOW COOKBOOKS

A Sausage Book

Helen Saberi

EXCELLENT PRESS
in association with
LUDLOW BOOKBINDERS

Excellent Press
9 Lower Raven Lane
Ludlow SY 8 1 BW

©2006, Helen Saberi and Excellent Press

Printed in the UK by Woolnough
Bookbinding Ltd, 2006

ISBN 1 900318 31 8

Recipes

Publisher's Note

Ludlow is a place where the sausage is fully appreciated. It must be the only town in England where you can order sausages online from the Mayor. In the town centre, four independent butchers flourish, each offering individual and special sausages and competing at the annual Food Festival, held in September, for the title of Sausage Champion. Undeterred by this abundant choice of suppliers in town, the intrepid itinerant sausage-maker Mr Tudge regularly brings his produce to the town market where he is received with enthusiasm. He is by no means the only maker from outside who sells sausages in the market.

For most cooks, even in Ludlow, the sausage is a food which is simply dealt with: it is sizzled on the barbecue, broiled under the grill, baked in the oven or unfashionably fried. Yet there are many more interesting ways to cook sausages from the plain traditional (Toad in the Hole) to the gourmet delicious (Ali-Bab's Sausages in White Wine).

This small book gives a feast of classic recipes old and new to be going on with as the first in our series of cookbooks published in celebration of Ludlow's success as a food town.

A sausage is typically a meat mixture, usually pork, mutton, or beef, which is chopped and stuffed into a tubular casing. A sausage was one of the first convenience foods going back to antiquity. It was a way of preserving the blood and minor bits and pieces of an animal. The sausage's very name preserves its preservative origins: it goes back to the Latin for 'salted', *salsus*. The Romans introduced into northern and western Europe the cylindrical sausage of spiced minced meat stuffed into a skin of animal intestine (casings).

However, as Alan Davidson explains in *The Oxford Companion to Food* (1999) meat is not a defining characteristic for there are fish sausages (also known since antiquity) and Glamorgan sausages are made from cheese and leeks. The cylindrical shape is also not essential. Some sausages are spherical, ovoid or flattish. Finally, not all sausages are made with casings. A casing is not essential and many types of sausages are shaped into cohesive rolls or patties and count as sausages because of their shape and composition.

Many different types of sausages are made in other parts of the world, including the numerous varieties of cured sausages on the Continent. But this book is mainly concerned with British sausages.

****

SAUSAGES OF BRITAIN

In the past British sausages were like those from the European Continent and were made more or less entirely of cured meat. Today pure pork sausages are still made here on a small scale but most British sausages now comprise fresh meat mixed with cereals.

SOME VARIETIES OF BRITISH SAUSAGES

OXFORD SAUSAGE

Dallas in *Kettner's Book of the Table* (1877) gives a rather witty introduction to this sausage followed by a recipe.

'It is not a comforting reflection that our two most ancient and renowned universities, with all their scholarship, all the wisdom of the classics to command, and all the heights of philosophy beneath their feet, have been able to add to the enjoyments of the table nothing more than an humble sausage. What is learning, what is science, if this be its farthest reach – to evolve only a sausage from the inner consciousness? Each University has one; but Oxford has certainly the best of it. Whereas both of these great schools chop logic and pork, Oxford in addition chops veal and the fat of beeves.

'Oxford Sausage. - Mince one pound each of prime young pork, veal, and the freshest beef fat, all cleared of skin and sinews; steep the crumb of a twopenny loaf in milk and water; grate a little zest of lemon, also a little nutmeg; chop a few sage leaves and some thyme; and pound a small quantity of long pepper and salt. Mix all together and press it down close in a pan for use. It may be stuffed in skins like other sausage meat; but is generally rolled out as wanted, and either fried in fresh butter of a fine brown colour or broiled over a clear fire. This is what ages of learning have taught the wise men of the Isis to fix upon as the only preparation of food to which the name of Oxford may worthily be linked.'

CAMBRIDGE SAUSAGE

This is what the same book has to say about the Cambridge sausage:

'The rivalry of the twin universities has extended to the table. Oxford has its sausage and its punch. Cambridge has its sausage and its punch too. But there is an originality in the Oxford preparations to which Cambridge can make no approach. The Oxford sausage is a crêpinette, can be made at home, and affords infinite scope for variety of flavour. The Cambridge sausage is always put into skins, and that is a business of itself which had better be left to the pork-butcher. There is therefore a uniformity about it which is a little too suggestive of mathematics.'

EPPING SAUSAGES

As can be seen from the above types of sausages are commonly named after a place. As with the Oxford sausage Epping sausages were also skinless and coated with eggs and crumbs.

Florence White in *Good Things in England* (1932) gives a recipe for these sausages dating from 1826.

This also is a recipe for skinless sausage and easy to make. It is quite simple to make any small quantity.

INGREDIENTS: Young pork 6 lb.; beef suet 6 lb.; sage leaves, a handful; some thyme, savory and marjoram; lemon 1, nutmegs 2; pepper, a spoonful; salt, a large spoonful; egg as much as will make it smooth.

Method

1. Put the pork free from skin, gristle and fat through a mincer, and pound it fine in a mortar.
2. Chop the beef suet very fine.
3. Shred sage leaves finely.
4. Spread the meat on a clean dresser [board] and shake the sage over it.
5. Shred the rind of the lemon very fine and throw it with some chopped sweet herbs on the meat.
6. Grate the nutmegs over it, powder with the pepper and salt.
7. Chop the suet finely and throw that over it.
8. Mix all well together, and put down close in a pot ready for use.
9. Then roll it up into sausages with as much egg as will make it smooth, and fry in clarified fat, or grill.

Glamorgan Sausages

Despite their name, Glamorgan sausages from Wales do not contain meat but are made of cheese, breadcrumbs, herbs and chopped onion or leek, mixed together and formed into sausage shapes or rissoles. They are fried and usually eaten with potatoes. These were the poor man's substitute for meat sausages.

175 g fresh breadcrumbs
100 g Caerphilly cheese, grated
1 small leek, washed and very finely chopped
15 ml chopped fresh parsley
large pinch of mustard powder
salt and pepper
2 eggs, separated
milk to mix
plain flour, or breadcrumbs
2 tablespoons vegetable oil or butter, or a mix of the two

Mix together the breadcrumbs, cheese, leek, parsley and mustard in a bowl and season to taste. Add 1 whole egg and 1 egg yolk and knead together, adding some milk if necessary to bind. Form the mixture into 8 rissoles or sausage shapes.

Beat the remaining egg white until frothy and dip the sausages into this and then roll in the flour or crumbs to coat. Now fry the sausages in the oil or butter until golden brown and cooked through.

KENTISH SAUSAGE MEAT

Eliza Acton in *Modern Cookery for Private Families* (1845) has a recipe for Kentish sausage-meat.

To three pounds of lean pork, add two of fat [pork], and let both be taken clear of skin [skin removed]. As sausages are lighter, though not so delicate, when the meat is somewhat coarsely chopped, this difference should be attended to in making them. When the fat and lean are partially mixed, strew over them two ounces and a half of dry salt, beaten to powder, and mixed with one ounce of ground black pepper, and three large tablespoonsful of sage, very finely minced. Turn the meat with the chopping-knife, until the ingredients are well blended. Test it before it is taken off the block, by frying a small portion, that if more seasoning be desired, it may at once be added. A full-sized nutmeg [grated], and a small dessertspoonful of pounded mace, would, to many tastes, improve it. This sausage-meat is usually formed into cakes, which, after being well floured, are roasted in a Dutch oven. They must be watched, and often turned, that no part may be scorched.

Lean of pork, 3 lb; fat 2 lb; salt, 2$\frac{1}{2}$ oz; pepper, 1 oz; minced sage, 3 large tablespoonsful.

OYSTER SAUSAGES

Sausages containing oysters are generally not heard of today. Mrs Cleland in her book *A New and Easy Method of Cookery* (1755) gave a recipe using Mutton and Beef, along with three half 'Mutchkins of Oysters' and flavouring with cloves and mace. Mrs Rundell's later recipe in her book *Domestic Economy* (c. 1842) is, however, easier to follow.

> Take a pound of veal and a score of oysters bearded, then pound the veal very finely in a mortar with a little suet, season with a little pepper, soak a piece of bread in the oyster liquor, pound, and add it with the oysters cut in pieces to the veal, beat up an egg to bind them together, and roll them into little lengths, like sausage; fry them in butter a delicate brown.

Dallas in *Kettner's Book of the Table* (1877) also gives a recipe for oyster forcemeat which is similar but no meat is involved just breadcrumbs, a dozen oysters, minced and butter, zest of lemon, parsley, some nutmeg and cayenne. He suggests using the balls as a stuffing for turkey but also adds 'It is also excellent as a stuffing for fish, such as John Dory.'

PORTUGUESE SAUSAGES

The popular 19th century author Mrs Rundell gave a recipe for Portuguese sausages. We have been unable to find how the name came about. The only remote connection is that they are seasoned with Spanish or red pepper and they are marinated in wine for eight days.

BOLOGNA SAUSAGES *(better known now as Polony)*

According to Laura Mason in *Traditional Foods of Britain* (1999) the name Polony may be a corruption of Polonia (Poland) or more probably Bologna. 'Whichever, polony has had over 300 years to develop a British identity, for Bologna or Polony sausage was popular in the 17th century (Wilson 1973)'. Two areas of Britain are particularly associated with polony. One, the spa town of Bath, was famous for this sausage in the past. The second area linked with them was Yorkshire, especially Sheffield. Recipes vary but basically polony is made from a mixture of lean and fat raw pork, chopped very fine and mixed with flour paste or rusk and seasonings according to individual recipes. This is stuffed into wide casings. They are boiled with red food colouring in the water which results in the characteristic bright red skin enclosing a pale pink meat.

CUMBERLAND SAUSAGES

These sausages from Cumberland have become very popular in the south of Britain. They contain a very high meat content of pork and pork fat, highly flavoured with spices and herbs. The sausages traditionally have a characteristic long unlinked coil shape.

SAVELOYS

Saveloys were very popular in Victorian Britain. They are a highly seasoned smoked sausage made of pork. The word Saveloy is an adaptation of the French *cervelas*, a medium-sized pork sausage of eastern France which is usually simmered in water or red wine. Sadly, nowadays in the words of John Ayto in *A Gourmet's Guide* (1994): '... the saveloy is often a distinctly dubious proposition, its traditional recipe of fine pork replaced by a less easily definable mixture frequently concealed behind a lurid red casing.'

BEAUVILLIERS' SAUSAGE

This sausage comes from the greatest Paris restaurateur of the early 19th century. Meg Dods (1829) gives the recipe :

Mince what quantity of fresh pork will be necessary; mix with it equal to a quarter of lard; add salt and fine spices; fill the skins and tie them; hang them in the smoke for three days; then cook them in *bouillon* for three hours, with salt, a clove of garlic, thyme, bay, basil, parsley, and young onions; when cold, serve upon a napkin.

SMOKED SCOTCH SAUSAGES

Meg's native Scottish sausage is a rougher type:

Smoked Scotch sausages, to keep and eat cold.-
Salt a piece of beef for two days, and mince it with suet. Season it highly with pepper, salt, onion, or eschalot. Fill a large well-cleaned ox-gut, plait it in links, and hang the sausage in the chimney to dry.* Boil it as wanted either a single link or altogether.

* Some of these sausages wont to be made when a Mart was killed: they formed an excellent article of supply for the hill, the moor, or the boat; and in the Hebrides and remote parts of the Highlands they still hold a favourite place in the wide open chimney.

BLACK PUDDINGS

Black puddings are usually displayed with the ends tied together to form a circle. They are made from pig's blood, trimmings of pork fat, a thickening agent such as oatmeal or bread, onions, and flavoured with herbs and spices. The mixture is put into prepared gut, tied up and then boiled. Once cooked they keep for several days and then may be re-boiled for serving hot, or cut into slices and fried. The Midlands and the North are particularly renowned for their black puddings. The best are said to come from Bury in Lancashire.

OTHER SAUSAGES

- Wiltshire sausages, which are seasoned with ginger.
- Lincolnshire, seasoned with sage and thyme.
- Manchester, with sage, cloves, nutmeg and ginger.
- Tomato sausage, a peculiar local variety which remains popular in the Midlands and Yorkshire. It is a normal British pork sausage coloured reddish with tomato puree.
- Chipolatas are thin, long sausages. They are also used as an accompaniment to the Christmas turkey, often wrapped round with bacon.
- Cocktail sausages are similar to chipolatas but much shorter. They are popular for snacks or for parties.
- Venison sausages.
- Wild Boar Sausages.

Many supermarkets now sell their own varieties with different flavourings and ingredients.

In Ludlow there are four independent butchers who offer a variety of high quality sausages. Their sausages include:

A H Griffiths:

- Pork, Leek and Stilton
- Shropshire Sizzlers (pork, peaches, Shropshire Blue cheese)
- Cumberland
- Traditional pork
- Cocktail sausages

Carters:

- Ludlow pork sausages in two sizes
- Venison and pork
- Pork and tomato
- Pork, onion, redcurrant and sage
- Pork, sun dried tomato and basil
- Mexican pork
- Pork, leek, apricot and wholegrain mustard
- Pork, honey and wholegrain mustard
- Shropshire tasty porkers
- Cumberland

Andrew Francis:

- Sweet chilli and fennel
- Welsh spicy leek
- Rare breed Berkshire Black
- Old English (pork, sage, thyme, rosemary and onion)
- Pork and leek
- Pork, sage and cider apple
- Pork, chive and paprika
- Pork, spring onion and ginger
- Cumberland
- Venison sausage
- Traditional pork

D W Wall:

- Farmhouse pork
- Pork, basil and sun dried tomato
- Shropshire Lad beer and mustard
- Rare breed pork and leek (80% meat and gluten free)
- Cumberland

By way of introduction on how to cook sausages, first of all a quote from Florence White who wrote the following advice in her book *Good Things in England* (1932). (Dr Kitchiner was the author of the *Cook's Oracle*, 1816):

DELICIOUS ENGLISH SAUSAGES

'Dr. Kitchiner says "Sausages are best when quite fresh made." The secret of frying sausages is:
1. To let them get hot very gradually, then they will not burst if they are quite fresh.
2. Do not prick them with a fork because this lets all their gravy out.
3. Dredge them lightly with flour, rubbing it smooth and discarding the loose flour.
4. Put a bit of butter or clarified dripping into a clean frying-pan.
5. As soon as it is melted (and before it gets hot) put in the sausages.
6. Shake the pan for a minute, and keep turning them but be careful not to prick or break them in so doing.
7. Fry them over a very slow fire till they are nicely browned all over.

N.B. 'Some over-economical cooks' Dr. Kitchiner says, 'insist that no butter or lard is required; the fat of the sausages being sufficient to fry them. We have tried it, - the sausages were partially scorched and had that pie-bald appearance that fried things have when sufficient fat is not allowed.'

(Poached eggs, pease-pudding, and mashed potatoes are agreeable accompaniments to sausages, and sausages are as welcome with boiled or roasted poultry or veal or boiled tripe, and are a convenient, easily digested and invigorating food for old folk and those whose teeth are not strong.)'

There are other ways of cooking sausages:

Grilled sausages: Heat the grill to hot, put the sausages on the grill rack and cook until one side is golden brown. Turn over and continue cooking, turning frequently for about 15 to 20 minutes, until the sausages are well browned.

Baked sausages: To my mind, a much easier way of cooking sausages. Heat the oven to 200°C, 400°F, gas mark 6. Put the sausages in a greased baking tin and cook for about 30 minutes turning or shaking the pan every now and again to ensure even cooking. If you like you can make what are called kilted sausages by wrapping rinded streaky bacon rashers round pairs of chipolatas or a sausage in which case reduce the oven temperature to 190°C, 375°F gas mark 5.

Sausage cakes: Mix 450 g sausage meat with 1 finely chopped onion and 1 teaspoon dried mixed herbs. Divide into 8 and form into round cakes or patties. Dust with a little flour. Heat about 25 g fat or oil in a pan and fry the cakes gently over a low heat for about 10 minutes, turning them over until crisp and brown on both sides.

All recipes serve four unless otherwise stated.

****

BANGERS N'MASH

The colloquial 'banger' is a synonym for the sausage, and probably came about because of the noise a sausage sometimes makes when being fried. This is the most well known of sausage dishes.

1 kg floury potatoes, peeled and cut into large cubes
75 g butter
100-150 ml milk
500 g sausages

Boil the potatoes in salted water until tender. Drain well. Add the butter, and mash well. Now add the milk bit by bit mashing well until you achieve the right creamy and fluffy consistency. Keep warm.

Grill, bake or fry the sausages.

Place the mashed potatoes in a serving dish and serve the sausages separately or arrange the sausage around or on top of the potatoes.

Serve with fried onion and gravy or a rich onion gravy.

****

VARIATIONS ON MASHED POTATO:

With celeriac:

225 ml water
1/2 teaspoon salt
black pepper
1/2 teaspoon marjoram
1/2 teaspoon grated lemon rind
450 g floury potatoes, peeled and chopped

450 g celeriac, peeled and sliced
1 onion, chopped
50 ml hot milk
75 g Cheddar cheese, grated

In a pan bring the water, salt, pepper, marjoram and lemon rind to the boil over a moderately high heat. Add the potatoes, celeriac and onion to the pan, reduce the heat to low and simmer for 20 to 25 minutes or until the vegetables are very tender. Remove from the heat and drain the vegetables. Discard the cooking liquid.

Puree the vegetables in a blender and transfer the puree back to the pan. Add the hot milk and the cheese to the vegetables and beat well with a wooden spoon until thoroughly mixed.

Spoon the pureed vegetables on to a warm serving dish and arrange the sausages on top.

With swede:

450 g floury potatoes, cubed	*hot milk*
450 g swede, cubed	*salt and pepper*
50 g butter	*grated cheese*

Boil the potatoes and swede together in water for about 10 to 15 minutes, until tender. Drain, add the butter and mix well. Add the hot milk, according to taste to make a soft but fluffy mashed potato mixture. Season with salt and pepper and sprinkle on a little grated cheese, if wished.

****

SAVOURY HEDGEHOG

While researching this book I came across a rather novel idea for lunch or tea for children on the theme of sausage and mash. It is called Savoury Hedgehog and appeared in *More Recipe Round-ups from Dairy Diaries* (1986-1990).

Prepare the mashed potatoes and sausages as on page 19 but shape the potatoes into a hedgehog shape on a flattish serving platter. Cut all the sausages in half except one. Arrange the halves like hedgehog spines. Cut the remaining sausage to make eyes and a snout. Serve with baked beans.

****

TOAD IN THE HOLE

250 g sausages
100 g plain flour
pinch of salt
1 egg
250 ml milk
50 g dripping, lard or oil

First of all make the batter. Mix the flour and salt in a basin, and make a hollow in the centre and drop in the egg.

Add the milk gradually, stirring with a wooden spoon until all the flour is worked in. Now beat well. Set to one side.

Place a little fat or oil in a Yorkshire pudding tin. Add the sausages and cook in a hot oven at 220°C, 425°F, gas mark 7 for about 10 minutes.

Remove from the oven and pour the batter over the partly cooked sausages and cook for a further 30 minutes or until the batter is set and the top is golden brown.

Serve with mashed potatoes (see pages 19 and 20), peas and gravy. English mustard is an optional accompaniment.

CUMBERLAND SAUSAGE WITH YORKSHIRE PUDDINGS

This is a variation on the theme of Toad in the Hole and Sausage and Mash, combining the two. Round Yorkshire puddings are made into which a Cumberland sausage is placed and the pudding is filled with gravy. This is served with mashed potatoes and peas.

4 individual Cumberland sausages

For the batter:
100 g plain flour
pinch of salt
1 egg, beaten
250 ml semi-skimmed milk

For the mashed potatoes:
1 kg floury potatoes, peeled and cut into large cubes
75 g butter
100-150 ml milk

First of all make the batter. Mix the flour and salt in a basin, and make a hollow in the centre and drop in the egg.

Add the milk gradually, stirring with a wooden spoon until all the flour is worked in. Now beat well. Set to one side.

Now make your mashed potatoes as follows:

Boil the potatoes in salted water until tender. Drain well. Add the butter, and mash in well with a potato masher. Now add the milk bit by bit mashing well until you achieve the right fluffy consistency. Keep warm.

Grill, bake or fry the sausages. Keep warm.

In a pre-heated oven (230°C, 450°F, Gas mark 8) melt 15 g dripping, lard or oil divided equally between four round Yorkshire pudding tins. Heat in the oven until a haze appears. Pour the batter in equal proportions into the tins. Return to the oven and bake for about 20 minutes until well risen and crispy brown edges.

Remove the puddings from the tins, place on individual plates, add a sausage to the centre of each pudding, fill with a little gravy and serve with mashed potatoes and peas. Serve extra gravy separately.

****

FRIED SAUSAGES AND APPLES

There is a long tradition of cooking sausages with apples. Here is an early recipe from Hannah Glasse's *The Art of Cookery Made Plain and Easy* (1747). Mrs Cleland, in her book *A New and Easy Method of Cookery* which was published in 1755, gives a suspiciously similar recipe but increases the amount of sausages to one pound. She also suggests that potatoes, thinly sliced could be a substitute for the apples. Both ladies add that 'stew'd cabbage or pease pudding' also go well with fried sausages.

Fry'd Sausages
Take half a Pound of Sausages, and six Apples; slice four about as thick as a Crown; cut the other two in Quarters, fry them with the Sausages of a fine light-brown; lay the Sausages in the Middle of the Dish, and the Apples round; garnish with the quarter'd Apples.

FRIED SAUSAGES AND APPLES

This is another recipe using apples. It comes from a little known and rare book entitled *A Friend in Need: English-Tamil Cookery Book* (3rd edition), compiled by the Ladies' Committee F.I.N.S. Women's Workshop, published in Madras in 1950.

The method of cooking the apples is slightly different and the dish is served with fried bread.

1 lb sausages
2 or 3 oz. dripping
A little flour
2 cooking apples
Parsley
A little milk
Fried bread

Heat the dripping in a frying pan, prick the sausages and fry in the pan until brown on all sides. Lift out and keep hot. Peel, core and slice the apples, dip them in a little milk and then flour and fry in the sausage pan, drain well and remove, fry small pieces of bread in the same pan. Serve the sausages and apples together surrounded by the fried bread and garnished with the fried parsley.

Plantains* may be used instead of apples.

*Plantain is the name given to varieties of the banana which are only suitable for cooking.

STUFFED APPLES AND SAUSAGE

Here is another slant on the theme of the popular combination of apples and sausage, also from the Ladies of Madras.

'Remove a little of the tops of apples allowing one for each person. Core and scoop out a little of the centre. Stuff with sausage meat and bake until tender. Very good served with roast duck.'

****

SAUSAGE EGGS

The following recipe for 'open plan' Scotch Eggs completes our choice from 1950s Madras.

1/2 lb sausage meat
4 eggs
1 oz butter
1 teaspoon chopped parsley

Butter 4 small moulds and line with sausage meat. Put in the oven for 15 to 20 minutes. Remove. Break eggs carefully, one into each mould and top each with a little butter. Cover with greaseproof paper, and return to oven until the egg is set. Sprinkle with fresh chopped parsley.

VEAL AND SAUSAGE PIE

Mrs Rundell, calling herself 'A Lady', first published *A New System of Domestic Cookery* in 1806, which was followed by numerous other editions over many years. In our edition of c. 1842 there is a recipe for Veal and Sausage Pie. (See page 13 for an explanation of Bologna.)

Cover a shallow dish with paste, lay a well-beaten veal cutlet at the bottom slightly seasoned, cover it with a Bologna sausage freed from the skin, and cut into slices; then add another cutlet and a layer of the Bologna sausage; cover the whole with paste, and put no water to it. The veal will give out sufficient gravy, while it will be rendered very savoury by the sausage. It is excellent eaten cold.

****

SAUSAGES AND CHESTNUTS

This recipe comes from Eliza Acton's book *Modern Cookery*, published in 1845. She describes it as an 'Entrée – An excellent dish – French'.

Roast, and take the husk and skin from forty fine Spanish chestnuts; fry gently, in a morsel of butter, six small flat oval cakes of fine sausage-meat, and when they are well browned, lift them out and pour into a saucepan, which should be bright in the inside, the greater part of the fat in which they have been fried; mix with it a large teaspoonful of flour, and stir these over the fire till they are well and equally browned; then pour in by degrees nearly half-pint of strong beef or veal broth, or gravy, and two glasses of good white wine; add a *small* bunch of savoury herbs, and as much salt and pepper, or cayenne, as will season the whole properly; give it a boil, lay in the sausages round the pan, and the chestnuts in the centre; stew them *very* softly for nearly an hour; take out the herbs, dish the sausages neatly and heap the chestnuts in the centre, strain the sauce over them and serve them very hot. There should be no sage mixed with the pork to dress thus.

Chestnuts roasted, 40; sausages, 6; gravy, nearly ½ pint; sherry or Madeira, 2 wineglassesful; stewed together from 50 to 60 minutes.

****

TRUFFLED SAUSAGES
(Saucisses aux Truffes)

Here is another Eliza Acton recipe. Truffles are a rather expensive delicacy now but garlic is given as a substitute.

With two pounds of the lean of young tender pork, mix one pound of fat, a quarter of a pound of truffles, minced very small, an ounce and a half of salt, a seasoning of cayenne, or quite half an ounce of white pepper, a nutmeg, a teaspoonful of freshly pounded mace, and a dessertspoonful or more of savoury herbs dried and reduced to powder. Test a morsel of the mixture; heighten any of the seasonings to the taste; and put the meat into delicately clean skins; if it be for immediate use, and the addition is liked, moisten it, before it is dressed, with one or two glassesful of Madeira. The substitution of a clove of garlic for the truffles, will convert these into *Saucisses à l'Ail*, or garlic sausages.

LADY LLANOVER'S WELSH SAUSAGES

This recipe comes from *The First Principles of Good Cookery* (1867) an eccentric but valuable work by Lady Llanover, one of the foremost activists in reviving the Welsh language and culture in the 19th century.

Quarter of a pound of roast or baked pork, quarter of a pound of baked veal, two ounces of cold boiled tongue, an ounce and a half of onions chopped very fine, an ounce and a quarter of sage, flour well, add pepper and salt to taste; pound well in a mortar, and make into very thin, short, round sausages; beat up one egg well, and glaze the sausages with it, then roll them in two ounces of fine bread crumbs, and fry in boiling-hot top fat (from soup stock) until the sausages are a fine golden brown: if they are at all greasy, put them on a soft hot cloth on a flat dish in a screen before the fire, and turn them on the cloth till they are perfectly dry, before serving.

N.B. - Where pork is used it can be baked in the same manner as directed for the fillet of veal [not given here]; but if no more is wanting than the quantity to make sausages, it is better to cut up a quarter of a pound of raw pork and a quarter of a pound of raw veal, and half a quarter of a pint of water and a little salt, which can be baked slowly in a double Ffwrn fach [a kind of steamer], or it can be stewed in a double saucepan till the meat is fit for eating. When it is not convenient to provide pork or veal, cold stewed beef, or indeed any cold meat, will make very good sausages, if pounded, with the addition of a little finely-chopped suet, and well flavoured with sage.

STEWED SAUSAGES

Francatelli, who was maitre d'hotel and chief cook to Queen Victoria and author of *The Modern Cook* and *The Cook's Guide* did not concern himself exclusively with grand royal cooking. He had a social conscience too, and produced *A Plain Cookery Book for the Working Classes* in 1852.

First, prick your sausages well all over with a fork, and soak them in very hot water, for two or three minutes to swell them out; next, roll them in flour, and fry them brown without overdoing them, as that renders them dry, and spoils them. When the sausages are done and put on a plate, fry some slices of bread, and put these on a dish; then put the sausages on the fried bread, and shake a spoonful of flour in the pan; add a pennyworth of chopped mixed pickles, a gill of water, and a little pepper and salt; give this gravy a boil up, and pour it over the sausages.

****

SAUSAGE DUMPLINGS

Francatelli also gives a recipe for sausage dumplings. You will need 12 sausages.

Make one pound of flour and two ounces of dripping, or chopped suet, into a firm paste, by adding just enough water to enable you to knead the whole together. Divide this paste into twelve equal parts, roll each of these out sufficiently large to be able to fold up one of the beef sausages in it, wet the edge of the paste to fasten the sausage securely in it, and, as you finish off each sausage dumpling, drop it gently into a large enough saucepan, containing plenty of *boiling* water, and when the whole are finished, allow them to boil gently by the side of the fire for one hour, and then take up the dumplings with a spoon free from water, on to a dish, and eat them while they are hot.

SAUSAGE AND KIDNEY

This recipe, which has been adapted slightly, comes from a useful little book *The Everyday Savoury Book* by Marie Worth which in her own words: 'It will be readily conceived that the task of producing 365 savoury dishes has been no easy one. (Not the modern idea of the "savoury," but what was *originally* meant by the word – "A Tasty Dish").'

4 small onions, finely chopped
250 g sausages
250 g kidneys (ox or lambs')
salt and pepper
250 ml stock
1 tablespoon butter
1 level tablespoon flour
mashed potatoes

Fry the onion in the butter for five minutes, stirring frequently. Cut the sausages in half lengthways, place them in a pan, slice the kidneys thinly and add to the onions in the pan. Season with salt and pepper, according to taste, and fry gently for a few minutes, turning carefully. (Do not overcook the kidneys too much, or they will be hard.) Add the stock, let the contents of the pan simmer for three minutes or so, then place the sausages and kidneys on a hot dish. Thicken the gravy with a small lump of butter, rolled in the flour. Simmer for a few minutes and pour over the kidneys and sausages.

Serve with a wall of fluffy mashed potatoes.

BAKED SAUSAGE AND TOMATO

Here is another recipe from *The Everyday Savoury Book* which has been slightly adapted. It makes a tasty lunch or supper dish.

250 g sausage meat
1 egg, well beaten
2 teaspoons finely chopped parsley
breadcrumbs
1 onion, finely chopped
3 tomatoes, cut in halves
250 g bacon
1 tablespoon butter
pepper to taste

Shape the sausage meat into six round flat cakes. Brush over with well beaten egg. Mix the parsley, breadcrumbs and onion together. Gently roll and coat the sausage cakes into this mixture. Season with pepper. Cut the bacon making into six pieces and place a piece on each of the sausage cakes. Top with half a tomato, the cut side downwards.

Melt the butter in a baking tin, place each cake in carefully and cook slowly in the oven at 180°C, 350°F, gas mark 4 for about fifteen minutes.

Serve with gravy and a border of mashed potatoes.

CUMBERLAND SAUSAGE IN BEER

This recipe comes from Laura Mason's book, *Farmhouse Cookery* (2005).

'Cumberland sausages should be full of coarse-cut meat and a bit of seasoning, and come in one long coil, not as links. They are excellent grilled or fried, but cooking them in beer produces a good gravy.'

25 g beef dripping or 2 tablespoons oil
500–600 g Cumberland sausage in one long coil
1 onion, peeled and sliced
1 tablespoon plain flour
300 ml beer, preferably not too bitter
salt and pepper

Try to use a frying pan or casserole in which the sausage will fit in a neat coil. Melt the dripping or oil and cook the sausage briefly on both sides, just enough to brown it. Remove it to a plate and add the onions to the fat and cook gently until soft but not brown. Sprinkle in the flour and stir well. Stir in the beer. Let it bubble and reduce a little. Add the sausage and cook very gently for 30 to 40 minutes. Taste the gravy and season if necessary, but the sausage will probably have provided enough salt. Serve with mashed potatoes.

SAUSAGE AND LEEK CASSEROLE
WITH CIDER

Ludlow is in the heart of cider country. Some of the fine pear trees which provided fruit for perry-making many years ago are still standing in old farms.

1 tablespoon vegetable oil
450 g pork sausages
1 large onion, chopped
3 leeks, washed and sliced in rounds
150 g mushrooms
3 tablespoons fresh parsley
150 ml Dunkerton's Dry Organic Cider
300 ml chicken stock
salt and pepper, to taste

Grill or bake the sausages, turning over from time to time until golden brown on all sides. Set to one side.

Heat the vegetable oil in an ovenproof casserole and add the onions, leeks and mushrooms. Fry gently for 3 to 5 minutes. Add the cider and stock. Bring to the boil and simmer for about 10 minutes.

Add the sausages, seasonings to taste and most of the parsley. Mix well, then cover and place in a preheated oven at 180°C, 350°F, gas Mark 4 for about 45 minutes.

Stir well before serving and sprinkle the remaining herbs on top.

Serve with mashed potatoes or crusty bread.

Sausages in White Wine

This delicious recipe, which has been slightly adapted, comes from the *Encyclopaedia of Practical Gastronomy* (1907) by the great Polish gastronome Henri Babinsky, who wrote in French under the name Ali Bab.

For six:

12 long thin chipolata sausages
400 ml white wine
100 g butter
1 medium onion, finely chopped or grated
40 g meat glaze or rich beef stock
4 teaspoons tomato puree, seasoned with herbs
4 teaspoons flour
slices of white bread

Melt 80 g of the butter in a casserole. Add the sausages and the onion. Cook together over a low heat for 10 to 15 minutes. Take out the sausages and keep warm in the oven.

Add the flour to the onions and mix well. Moisten with the wine and bring to the boil. Reduce. Now add the stock and tomato puree. Simmer and reduce again.

Strain and finish the sauce by whisking in the remaining butter.

Arrange the sausages on some canapés made with slices of fried bread. Coat with the sauce.

SAUSAGE AND TOMATO CASSEROLE

1 tablespoon vegetable oil
8 chipolatas or sausages
1 small onion, finely sliced
1 or 2 apples, peeled, cored and sliced
8 rashers rindless smoked streaky bacon
225 g tomatoes, sliced
225 g fresh peas
1 tablespoon fresh parsley
a little stock or water

Heat the oil over a medium heat in a large casserole.

Wrap each sausage in a rasher of bacon, then fry gently, turning regularly, for 5 to 10 minutes, until lightly browned on all sides. Arrange the onions, apples, tomatoes and peas in layers on top of the sausages and bacon. Add stock or water and place in a preheated oven and cook for 30 to 40 minutes at 200°C, 400°F, gas mark 6. Remove from the oven and stir well. Sprinkle with parsley before serving.

Serve with mashed potatoes and/or crusty bread.

SAUSAGES WITH SPINACH AND POTATOES

450 g sausages
2 tablespoons oil
450 g spinach, washed
4 spring onions, finely sliced
1/2 teaspoon ground fenugreek, optional
1 tablespoon fresh coriander, finely chopped
1 small onion
1 celery stick
200 g canned cherry tomatoes
150 ml vegetable stock
450 g potatoes, cooked, then sliced thinly
salt and pepper to taste

Brown the sausages in the frying pan or oven, then keep warm.

Heat 1 tablespoon of oil in a large saucepan and over a medium heat fry the spring onions with the fenugreek until softened. Do not burn. Add the spinach and the coriander. Stir well then cover with a lid and cook over a low heat for about 5 minutes, until just wilted. Drain well, reserving the liquid, then chop and season with salt and pepper. Spread over the base of an oiled 1.75 litre ovenproof dish. Place the sausages on the spinach.

Heat the other 1 tablespoon of oil in the large frying pan, add the onion and celery and fry until softened. Add the tomatoes and stir well. Add the stock and reserved liquid from cooking the spinach and bring to the boil, then simmer for 5 minutes. Season with salt and pepper, according to taste.

Pour the vegetables over the sausages and spinach. Arrange the potatoes over the top. Cook in a preheated oven, 190°C, 375°F, gas mark 5, for 30 minutes until the potatoes are golden brown. Serve hot.

Sausage and Turnip Stew

Venison sausages are good for this stew.

450 g sausages
3 tablespoons vegetable oil
1 large onion, chopped
450 g turnip, peeled and chopped into 2.5 cm cubes
50 g brown sugar
1 teaspoon ground ginger
1 teaspoon ground coriander
salt and pepper

Bake or grill the sausages until golden brown on all sides. Set to one side.

Heat the vegetable oil in a large ovenproof casserole and add the onions. Fry over a medium heat until soft and golden brown. Now add the chopped turnip and fry until brown. Add the ginger, coriander, sugar and salt and pepper to taste. Stir well and add about 100 ml of water. Bring to the boil, then simmer for about 10 minutes. Add the sausages to the vegetables in the pan and simmer for about another 15 to 20 minutes.

The sauce should be quite thick and the oil will separate out when the sauce is cooked.

DUBLIN CODDLE
(Sausages and Onions in Milk)

I have found two recipes for this traditional Dublin dish. According to Monica Sheridan in her book, *The Art of Irish Cooking* (1965):

'This is a dish that is eaten by families who have lived for generations in Dublin and who look upon the city as their local village. Sean O'Casey ate Dublin Coddle and Brendan Behan's mother still makes it. Dean Swift ate it in the Deanery of St. Patrick's Cathedral in the eighteenth century. ...

'It is eaten especially on Saturday night when the men come home from the pubs.'

She added at the end of the recipe that it was 'always washed down with draughts of Irish stout.'

The second recipe I found in Sheila Hutchins' book, *English Recipes and Others* (this would be one of the *Others*). I have taken the liberty of combining the two.

6–8 servings

450 g sausages
450 g onions, peeled and sliced
6 slices of bacon
4 or 5 floury potatoes, peeled and cut in 2 or 3 pieces
450 ml milk

Put the sausages in a stewpan with the sliced onions, the bacon and the potatoes. Cover with the milk, adding a little water if necessary.

Simmer for about 40 minutes, until the potatoes, onions, sausages etc are cooked and the milk has reduced to a thick and savoury onion sauce. Season with salt and pepper, if necessary.

SAUSAGE CASSEROLE WITH SWEET PEPPERS AND MUSHROOMS

8–12 sausages
2 tablespoons vegetable oil
2 large onions, peeled and finely chopped
1 large green pepper, de-seeded and chopped
100-170 g mushrooms, sliced
2 cloves of garlic, peeled and crushed
1 can (400g) chopped tomatoes
1 teaspoon dried oregano or basil, optional
salt and black pepper

Preheat the oven to 180°C, 350°F, gas mark 4.

Fry the sausages gently in a large casserole in the oil turning occasionally until golden brown on all sides. Remove the sausages and keep warm. Now add the chopped vegetables (onion, green pepper, mushrooms, garlic and chopped tomatoes). Fry gently for a couple of minutes and sprinkle on the oregano or basil and a little ground black pepper. Cover with the lid and place in the pre-heated oven for about 30 minutes. At this point add the sausages and put back in the oven for a further 20 to 30 minutes.

Serve with plain white rice or pasta.

SAUSAGE CURRY

For the sausages:
450 g pork sausagemeat
1 small onion, finely chopped
small piece of ginger, peeled and grated
1 small clove of garlic, peeled and crushed
seasoned flour
25 g ghee or vegetable oil

For the curry:
1 large onion, chopped
25 g ghee or vegetable oil
1 tablespoon curry powder
4 tomatoes, cut into small pieces
200 ml strained yoghurt

Mix the sausagemeat with the onion, garlic and ginger, and form into small sausage shapes. Toss lightly in a little seasoned flour. Heat the ghee or oil and fry the sausages in a pan gently until lightly browned. Remove them from the pan and keep warm.

In the same pan add the ghee or vegetable oil and fry the onion until soft and golden brown. Stir in the curry powder and fry for a few minutes. Add the tomatoes and mix well in the curry mixture. Add the sausages and a little water or stock if necessary. Cover and simmer gently until the ghee or oil separates out. Add the strained yoghurt, stir well to blend the flavours.

Serve with rice.

Sausage Paprika

450 g beef or pork sausages
1–2 tablespoons corn oil
2 onions, peeled and chopped
1 garlic clove, crushed
1 large green pepper, deseeded and thinly sliced
1 can chopped tomatoes
1 tablespoon paprika pepper
strained yoghurt or cream
salt

Grill the sausages until lightly browned, turning frequently for even cooking. Cut in half and keep warm.

Fry the onions in a casserole in the corn oil for about five minutes until they are becoming soft and golden brown. Now add the sliced green pepper and add the paprika. Fry further for a couple more minutes. Add the tomatoes, sausages and salt, according to taste. Cook slowly over a medium heat for about 20 to 30 minutes.

Remove from the heat and stir in enough yoghurt or cream to make a creamy sauce. Stir well to blend and reheat but do not boil.

SAUSAGE AND BEAN CHILLI

2 tablespoons vegetable oil
450 g sausages, preferably beef
1 large onion, skinned and finely chopped
1 green bell pepper, sliced
1 can (400 g) red kidney beans, drained
227 g can chopped tomatoes
1 tablespoon tomato puree
1 tablespoon vinegar
1 teaspoon sugar
1 tablespoon chilli seasoning powder
salt to taste

Heat the oil in a large flameproof casserole and fry the sausages gently for about 5 minutes until brown, turning frequently. Remove the sausages and keep warm.

Add the onions and peppers to the casserole and fry until soft. Drain off any excess fat. Return the sausages to the casserole, cut into bit sized pieces. Add the tomatoes. Mix the tomato puree, vinegar, sugar and chilli seasoning to a paste and add to the casserole. Stir to mix the ingredients together.

Cover and simmer gently for about 10 minutes, then add the beans. Cook for a further 10 to 15 minutes or until the sausages are tender and all the flavours have blended. Season with salt if required.

Serve with jacket potatoes or crusty bread.

SAUSAGE AND POTATO PIE

S ome cooked peas and carrots may be added to the dish for added colour and flavour before topping with the mashed potato.

450 g sausage meat or pork sausages
1 tablespoon vegetable oil
2 onions, chopped
450 ml beef stock
2 tablespoons fresh mixed herbs or 1 teaspoon dried sage
or mixed herbs
750 g floury potatoes, peeled and cut in cubes
75 g butter
milk
1 egg, beaten
salt and pepper to taste

Heat the oil and fry the sausages for about 6 minutes over a medium heat, turning occasionally until browned.

Add the onion, fry a little and then add the stock. Add the herbs. Bring to the boil and simmer for a couple of minutes.

Transfer to a casserole or ovenproof dish.

Boil the potatoes and cook until soft. Drain and add the butter mashing well. Slowly add enough milk and mash and beat to make fluffy mashed potatoes. Add seasonings.

Spread the mashed potatoes over the sausages to make the 'pie' topping. Brush with the beaten egg and make a pattern with a fork on the top. Place in a preheated oven at 200°C, 400°F, gas mark 6 for about half an hour, until golden on top.

VENISON SAUSAGES WITH BRAISED RED CABBAGE

This makes a hearty winter dish.

Serves 6

12 venison sausages
oil for frying
1 kg red cabbage
2 medium onions, skinned and sliced
2 cooking apples, peeled, cored and chopped
2 level teaspoons sugar
salt and black pepper
bouquet garni or bayleaf
2 tablespoons water
2 tablespoons red wine vinegar or red wine
25 g butter

First of all make the braised red cabbage.

Shred the cabbage finely, discarding any discoloured outside leaves and coarse stems. Layer the cabbage in a large casserole with the onions, apples, sugar and seasoning. Put the bouquet garni in the centre and pour the water and vinegar over. Cover tightly and cook in the oven at 200°C, 400°F, gas mark 6 for 1 hour. Remove the lid and continue cooking for about 30 minutes, until the liquid is evaporated. Add the butter and mix with the cabbage at the end of the cooking time.

Towards the end of the cooking time of the cabbage, fry or bake the sausages in the oil.

Place the cabbage in a deep serving dish either topped or surrounded by the sausages. I usually serve with scalloped potatoes.

LENTILS WITH SAUSAGES

A nother tasty recipe from Ali-Bab.

1 lb large lentils
1 lb ham
½ lb long, flat sausages or chipolatas
2 large carrots
2 small onions
1 small turnip
1 bouquet garni
salt and pepper

Carefully pick over the lentils and remove any stones. Wash them. Put the lentils in a saucepan with cold water and bring it to a boil. Add the carrots, onions, turnip, bouquet garni and salt and pepper. Cook these together.

At the same time braise the ham which has been seasoned with salt and pepper and puree it.

Remove the carrots, onions, turnip and bouquet garni. Drain the lentils. Mix them with the ham puree and cooking liquid. Let these simmer together for 30 minutes.

Grill the sausages. Spoon the lentils on to a platter and garnish with the sausages.

DEVILLED SAUSAGES

'Devilled', to devil, or devilling, is a culinary term which first appeared as a noun in the 18th century, and then in the early 19th century as a verb meaning to cook something with fiery hot spices or condiments.

This recipe has been inspired by a recipe in a rather witty, but nevertheless instructive and very practical book on country cooking, entitled *Countryman's Cooking* by W. M. W. Fowler (1965). His recipe was for devilled turkey drumsticks but here has been adapted using sausages.

Serves 3 to 4

1 oz butter
1/4 teaspoon each of Cayenne pepper, curry powder,
black pepper and a pinch of ginger.
3 teaspoons Worcestershire sauce
a little vinegar
450 g pork sausages

Mix together the butter, cayenne pepper, curry powder, black pepper, ginger and make into a paste with the Worcestershire sauce and a little vinegar. Spread this mixture over the sausages and fry gently turning frequently until well cooked. Or, bake in a hot oven at 200°C, 400°F, gas mark 6 for about 40 minutes, turning frequently to ensure even cooking.

SAUSAGES IN BARBECUE SAUCE

This recipe is flexible. Use English mustard if you wish a 'hotter' flavour. Instead of cooking the sausages in the sauce you could make up the sauce separately, fry or grill the sausages and serve separately.

vegetable oil
12 skinless sausages
1 onion, sliced finely
1 tablespoon cornflour
300 ml water
1 teaspoon Dijon or English mustard (made up)
1 teaspoon paprika pepper
2 tablespoons vinegar
2 tomatoes, chopped or sliced
salt and pepper

Heat the oil in a frying pan which has a lid or a casserole over a medium heat. Add the sausages and fry quickly to brown. Remove from the pan. Now add the onion to the pan and fry until golden and soft. Stir in the cornflour and fry briskly to brown. Now add the water gradually and the other ingredients, stirring constantly until the sauce comes to the boil and thickens. Season with salt and pepper, according to taste. Add the sausages, cover the pan and simmer gently for about 20 minutes.

SAUSAGE KEBABS
WITH CORIANDER CHUTNEY

T hese sausage-shaped kebabs are called *shami* or *lola* kebabs in Afghanistan.

makes approx 24

700 g best minced lamb or beef
4 medium potatoes
1 large onion, grated or finely chopped
1 egg
1/2-1 tablespoon chickpea flour
2 teaspoons ground coriander seeds
2 teaspoons powdered dill weed
1 teaspoon turmeric
salt and red pepper to taste

Peel, wash and boil the potatoes until soft and then mash them.

Combine the minced lamb, mashed potatoes, onion and all the other ingredients, including salt and pepper to taste. Mix thoroughly and knead until the mixture becomes smooth and a bit sticky.

Form into sausage-sized shapes and then fry in deep, hot oil. When sealed on all sides, reduce the heat to medium and cook gently until the kebabs are cooked through and golden brown on all sides.

Garnish with tomatoes, spring onion and lemon wedges and serve with nan or pitta bread and coriander chutney (see next page).

CORIANDER CHUTNEY

makes about a 1 lb jar

225 g fresh coriander (not the lower stems or roots)
10-25 g hot green chillies, seeds removed and finely chopped
10-25g garlic, peeled and chopped
25 g walnuts
25 g sugar
225 ml lemon juice or white wine vinegar
2 teaspoons salt
25g raisins (optional)

Grind the coriander, green chillies, garlic and walnuts in a blender, making sure that they are mixed thoroughly. Add the sugar to the lemon juice or vinegar and again mix well. Add this to the coriander mixture, with the salt and raisins, mix well and leave in a cool place.

The chutney can be put into a clean jar (or jars), screw on the lid and kept for a few days in the refrigerator.

SAUSAGE KEBABS WITH
RED PEPPER CHUTNEY

2 small red onions
12 speciality sausages
a little vegetable oil
parsley or coriander

For the chutney:

4 red bell peppers
2 hot red chillies
4-8 cloves of garlic

150 ml wine vinegar
75 g sugar (or to taste)
1 teaspoon salt

Cut the onions into six wedges. Thread three of the sausages through the middle on to wooden or metal skewers, but placing an onion wedge between each sausage. Continue with the remaining sausages and onion wedges in the same way. Brush the onions and sausages with a little vegetable oil.

Now make the chutney.

Wash the bell peppers, then dry them well. De-seed them and chop them up roughly. De-seed the hot chillies and chop them roughly, taking care in handling them. Peel the cloves of garlic and roughly chop. Place the peppers and the chillies in a blender with the garlic and blend. Try not to blend too much and leave the mixture a little 'chunky'. If you do blend for too long the chutney will be watery. Add the sugar, salt and vinegar according to taste. Mix well and leave in a cool place. (The chutney can be placed in jars and kept for up to a month in the refrigerator.)

Preheat the barbecue and cook the sausages, turning from time to time to cook evenly, until cooked through and evenly brown. The sausages can also be cooked under a preheated medium grill in the same fashion.

Garnish with some fresh parsley or coriander and serve with the chutney and fresh nan bread.

SAUSAGE CARTWHEEL

My sister gave me this recipe. She used to make it for her children when they had friends for tea. She also told me that grown-ups liked it too.

175g penne or fusilli pasta shapes
40 g butter
4 level tablespoons cornflour
568 ml milk
salt and pepper
100-150 g mature cheddar cheese, grated
8 chipolata sausages
4 tablespoons frozen garden peas
tomatoes for garnishing

First of all make the cheese sauce.

Melt the butter in a pan, stir in the flour and cook for 2 to 3 minutes, making a roux. Remove the pan from the heat and slowly stir in the milk. Return to the heat and, stirring continuously, thicken and bring to the boil. Stir in the cheese and the seasonings. Keep warm.

Fry or grill the chipolatas until cooked through and golden brown. Keep warm.

Cook the peas in boiling water for about 5 minutes. Keep warm.

Cook the pasta according to the instructions on the packet. Drain well. Now place the pasta into a deepish dish and cover with the sauce. Place the chipolatas on top of the pasta in a cartwheel design. In between the spokes place some peas. In the centre of the wheel, place half a tomato, cut side up. Round the edge of the cartwheel decorate with slices of tomato which have been halved.

SAUSAGE OMELETTE WITH LEEKS

T his recipe is based on an Afghan one for what is known there as *kuku* or *khagina*. These are very similar to *frittata*, the Spanish *tortilla* and the Middle Eastern *eggah*.

225 g chipolata sausages
3 tablespoons vegetable oil for frying
6 eggs
225 g leeks
1 bunch spring onions
2 medium tomatoes
1 green chilli, optional
1 teaspoon baking powder
2 teaspoons flour
salt and pepper
1 tablespoon fresh coriander

First of all fry the chipolatas in 1 tablespoon oil until golden on all sides in a round, deep frying pan of about 25 cm diameter which has a lid. Cut each chipolata in two. Remove from the pan and keep warm.

Beat the eggs in a large bowl. Cut off the hard green ends and remove the outer leaves from the leeks. Wash thoroughly and chop into small pieces. Do the same with the spring onions. Chop the tomatoes roughly and the chilli finely (first removing the seeds). Add all these ingredients to the beaten egg. Add the baking powder and flour. Mix well and season to taste with salt and pepper.

Heat 2 tablespoons of oil in the deep frying pan and pour the egg mixture over the hot oil. Reduce the heat to medium, add the sausages evenly to the egg mixture and cover with a lid and cook for about 15 minutes until the bottom of the omelette is browning and the vegetables are beginning to set in the egg mixture.

Now turn the omelette over. This can be tricky and the best way is to remove the pan from the heat, place a plate on top and then carefully turn the frying-pan upside down, then slip the omelette back into the pan on the other side.

Cook slowly over a medium heat for a further 10 to 15 minutes. Take care not to overcook the omelette, it should remain soft and not become leathery.

(Some people find it easier to brown the top of the omelette under the grill until the omelette is cooked through.)

Garnish with the fresh coriander and serve with fresh bread.

SAUSAGE AND PASTA SALAD

S ausages are very versatile and also go well in salads.

450 g sausages
olive oil
125 g pasta (penne, fusilli or tri-colour twists)
1/2 red sweet pepper, sliced or chopped
1/2 green sweet pepper, sliced or chopped
4 spring onions, sliced finely diagonally
2 celery stalks, chopped
1 apple, peeled, cored and sliced thinly or diced
3 tablespoons mayonnaise
small bunch basil, roughly torn
salt and pepper to taste

Fry the sausages over a medium heat in a little olive oil turning frequently to cook and brown evenly. Leave to cool.

Cook the pasta in plenty of boiling water according to the instructions on the packet. Rinse in cold water, drain and add the olive oil from cooking the sausages.

Slice or cut the sausages into bite-sized pieces and add to the pasta in a bowl. Add the peppers, spring onions, celery, apple and basil. Spoon in the mayonnaise and mix well. Add salt and pepper to taste.

Serve chilled for a buffet supper, or as part of a summer's barbecue.

POTATO SALAD WITH SAUSAGES

Sausages go brilliantly with potato salad. Use a British sausage of your choice or perhaps some frankfurters.

Serves 6

1 kg new potatoes, scraped
450 g sausages
3 tablespoons vegetable oil
1 1/2 tablespoons wine vinegar
50 g gherkins, finely chopped, optional
6 spring onions, finely sliced or chopped
a handful of cooked peas, optional
1-2 tablespoons mayonnaise
2 boiled eggs, each cut into four
parsley to garnish

Cook the potatoes in boiling salted water for about 10 minutes until just cooked but still firm. Drain and leave to cool in the pan. Cut in halves or dice when cool enough.

Cook the frankfurters or grill the sausages. Slice or chop each sausage into bite-sized pieces.

Mix together the oil and vinegar and salt and pepper (cayenne or paprika makes a nice change, or even a little curry powder) to taste. Pour over the potatoes in the pan. Add the gherkins, spring onions, peas and the sausages. Mix carefully but well to combine ingredients. Spoon over enough mayonnaise according to taste and mix again.

Serve in a large bowl or on a large serving dish, garnished with the hard-boiled eggs and sprinkled with the parsley.

SCOTCH EGGS

These are hard-boiled eggs encased in sausage meat or forcemeat and then fried. They are a popular snack, often taken on picnics. The Scottish origin is unclear but Meg Dods has a rather nice recipe using grated ham and anchovies and serving them with a gravy separately in her *Cook and Housewife's Manual* (1826) given below, followed by a modern version.

Scotch eggs.- Five eggs make a dish. Boil them hard as for salad. Peel and dip them in beat egg, and cover them with a forcemeat made of grated ham, chopped anchovy, crumbs, mixed spices &c. Fry them nicely in good clarified dripping, and serve them with a gravy-sauce separately.

****

4 eggs, hard-boiled
2 level teaspoons seasoned flour
Worcestershire sauce, or
2 teaspoons mixed herbs with a pinch of black or red pepper
225 g sausage meat
1 egg beaten
dry breadcrumbs
cooking fat or vegetable oil

Dust the eggs with the seasoned flour. Add a few drops of Worcestershire sauce or the mixed herbs to the sausage meat and divide it into 4 equal portions. Form each quarter into a flat cake and work it round an egg, making it as even as possible, to keep the egg a good shape and making sure there are no cracks in the sausage meat. Brush with beaten egg and toss in breadcrumbs. Heat the fat or oil in a deep fryer to a temperature of 180°C or in a deep pan until a cube of bread browns in 30 seconds. Carefully put in the eggs, 2 at a time frying for about 5 or 6 minutes, turning once, until they are a deep golden brown. (It is important that as the sausage meat is raw that the frying should not be too quick, leaving the outside to cook too quickly, leaving the inner meat undercooked.) Remove and drain on kitchen paper.

As with the Meg Dods recipe above these can be served hot with gravy or a tomato sauce or served cold as part of a salad or picnic.

****

PIGS IN BLANKETS

A favourite of children who like to make these themselves with the trimmings of left over pastry. The number of sausages you need depends on the amount of pastry you have, so this is a very vague recipe.

Pastry trimmings
Sausages
1 egg, beaten

Roll out your pastry trimmings into strips. Brush with beaten egg and wrap around each sausage. Place on a baking tray, glaze with beaten egg and bake in a preheated oven at 200°C, 400°F, gas mark 6 for approximately 15 to 20 minutes.

SAUSAGE LOAF

500 g sausage meat
1 onion, finely chopped
1 egg, beaten
handful of fresh herbs, chopped
black pepper or spices to taste
10 tablespoons breadcrumbs
10 tablespoons grated cheese

Mix well the onion and egg into the sausage meat. Add some fresh herbs with extra seasoning such as black pepper or other spices, according to taste. Grease a loaf tin and put in the sausage mixture. Top with the breadcrumbs and grated cheese mixed. Spread over the top of the sausage mixture.

Bake in a oven at 180°C, 350°F, gas mark 4 for about an hour.

Remove from the oven and allow to cool and set. Carefully remove the loaf from the tin and cut into slices.

Garnish with sliced tomatoes and cucumber, or according to fancy.

Sausage Rolls

T he final recipe in this little book is for that all-time favourite snack, the sausage roll. Ready-made rough puff pastry can be substituted.

200 g plain flour
½ teaspoon salt
125 g lard (or lard and margarine mixed)
cold water to mix, approx 100 ml
200 g sausage meat or skinless sausages
beaten egg or milk

First of all make the Rough Puff pastry.

Mix the flour and salt and then add the fat which should be cut into small pieces. Stir with a knife, then mix to a stiff paste with water.

Roll out on a floured surface to a narrow strip, then fold in three, turn one of the open ends towards you and roll out again. Repeat this process three times.

Leave the pastry to cool and rest in a refrigerator for about half an hour before making the sausage rolls.

Now roll out the pastry again to a long strip about 7.5 cm wide. Take the sausage meat and roll it with floured hands into one long 'sausage', as long as the pastry strip. Place on the edge of the pastry and roll up enclosing the 'sausage'. Dampen the edges and seal well.

Cut into the required lengths (about 2 cms is usual) and place on a baking try. Brush with the beaten egg or milk and make three cuts on the top.

Bake in a hot oven at 230°C, 450°F, gas mark 8 for about 20 minutes until golden brown.

Books Consulted:

The Dairy Book of British Food, Ebury Press, London , 1988

A Friend in Need: English-Tamil Cookery Book (3rd edn), FINS Women's Workshop, Madras , 1950

[Glasse, Hannah], *The Art of Cookery Made Plain and Easy*, by 'A Lady' (1747), facsimile reprint, Prospect Books, Totnes, 1995

[Rundell, Mrs], *A New System of Domestic Cookery*, new edn., John Murray, c.1842

Acton, Eliza, *Modern Cookery for Private Families*, Longman, Green, Longman and Roberts, 1845

Ali-Bab, *Encyclopaedia of Practical Gastronomy* (translated by Elizabeth Benson), McGraw-Hill, New York, 1974

Ayto, John, *A Gourmet's Guide – Food and Drink from A to Z*, OUP, Oxford , 1994

Cleland, Elizabeth, *A New and Easy Method of Cookery* (1755) facsimile reprint, Prospect Books, Totnes, Devon, 2005

Dallas, E S, *Kettner's Book of the Table* (1877) , Centaur Press, London, 1968

Davidson, Alan, *Oxford Companion to Food*, OUP, Oxford, 1999

Dods, Mistress Margaret (Meg), *The Cook and Housewife's Manual* (1829), 4th edn, facsimile reprint, Rosters Ltd, London, 1988

Fowler, W, *Countryman's Cooking*, Arlington Books, London, 1965

Francatelli, Charles Elmé, *A Plain Cookery Book for the Working Classes* (1852) reprint, The Scolar Press, Ilkley, 1977

Hartley, Dorothy, *Food in England*, Macdonald, London, 1954

Hutchins, Sheila, *English Recipes*, Methuen, London, 1967

Llanover, Lady, The Right Hon., *The First Principles of Good Cookery* (1867), facsimile reprint , Brefi Press, Dyfed, 1991

Mason, Laura, *Farmhouse Cookery*, The National Trust, London, 2005

Mason, Laura with Catherine Brown, *Traditional Foods of Britain*, Prospect Books, London, 1999

Sheridan, Monica, *The Art of Irish Cooking*, Gramercy, New York, 1965

White, Florence, *Good Things in England*, Jonathan Cape, London, 1932

The WI and Smith, Michael, *A Cook's Tour of Britain*, Will Books, London, 1984

Worth, Marie,*The Everyday Savoury Book*, Stanley Paul, London, n.d.